# HEAVY HORSES

# HEAVY HORSES

## EDWARD HART

B T BATSFORD LTD · LONDON

Frontispiece
*Tommy Gibson
adjusts harness on his
black Shires. The
white face marking is
known as the 'blaze'.*

## Acknowledgments

I should like to thank the following for their co-operation:
Ike Bay, Colin Fry, Bruce A. Roy and Paul Spoonley. I am specially indebted to Lee Weatherley. Thanks also to my wife Audrey for compiling the index, and to Gillian Scott for typing the manuscript.

Acknowledgment for the photographs is due as follows: Arthur Ackermann and Son: page 50: E. J. Anderton: page 9; Clydesdale Horse Society of the Dominion of New Zealand Inc: page 44; Audrey Hart: pages 8 (top), 10, 14, 18, 19, 22, 23, 25, 26, 31, 32, 38, 39, 40, 41, 45, 47, 51, 52, 54, 55, 56, 57, 58; Brian Hawley: page 16; *The Northern Echo:* page 37; J. Smith: page 17; Lee Weatherley: frontispiece, pages 6, 8 (bottom), 11, 12, 15, 21, 24/5, 27, 29, 30, 33, 34, 36, 42, 46, 49, 53, 58/9, 60.

*Edward Hart*

First published 1981
©Edward Hart 1981

ISBN 0 7134 3494 0

Phototypeset by Typewise Ltd., Wembley.

Printed in Hong Kong.
for the publishers B T Batsford Ltd,
4 Fitzhardinge Street, London W1H 0AH

# Contents

### The Shire Stallion

Between wild-flower ramparts
Crowned with the almond-scented gold
    of gorse,
Coronets and pasterns flinging snowy
    feather,
Shawl mane flying free,
He filled the lane with nuptial Majesty.

At bud and berry, dwarf Pan-faced Ishmael
By his side, he passed on through
A century of Mares, his girth and gleam,
The power of wheat-sack cruppers,
His oaken might of shin and cannon bone
The acre-taming sinews of his heart.

Now, as high summer gilds the pavilions,
Pedestal hooves lifted high with majestic
    sweetness,
Grand gleaming scion of the titans' age,
He Lords it again, in the Rings,
The awe and draw of thousands.

*John L. Jones*

# Horses and Horsemen

In the horse world the heavy breeds are quite distinctive. Clydesdale, Percheron, Shire and Suffolk are so different from the hot-blooded hunter or the nimble pony that they almost appear to belong to another species. The men – and women – who handle them are different too, and may love deeply their massive charges without necessarily having much interest in other types of horse.

'Once a heavy horseman, always a heavy horseman' is a truism that has been proved time and again. Standing beside the show ring, groups of leather-faced men watch the proceedings and claim that they in their day worked with the great horses. I have yet to meet one of them who regretted those years.

Most of them have reached middle age or beyond, for over thirty years have passed since the horse was the main source of power on farms and for city haulage. In the ten years following World War II, new and comparatively cheap motor lorries and tractors combined with low-priced fuel made the heavy horse seem uneconomic. In the 1960s it had become a rarity, kept on by a few devotees regarded as sentimental cranks by their fellow farmers. Brewery firms, who could afford to indulge their tastes and so gain from the advertising afforded, kept on dedicated and trusted horsemen until retirement; they also helped save the heavy.

That they did so was fortunate for the rest of us. The heavy horse survived, but only just.

Very, very few were being bred. Once they had been a mainstay of the rural economy, worked and quietened on the land for a couple of years before being sold in their thousands to the towns as nicely trained five-year-olds.

Then, in 1970, a party of forty North American heavy horsemen came to Britain, met breeders, saw horses at home and in the show-ring, and left substantial orders and promise of more. At last there was a market. The British stockbreeder can breed anything if there is money in it, and the heavy horse ceased to be a nostalgic hobby and reappeared as a business.

Enterprising show secretaries realise that as a crowd puller the heavy horse is unmatched. It has become the exhibition animal par excellence. It surpasses the show jumper in popular appeal, as is evident when the two classes are staged side-by-side at such events as Doncaster's Pageant of the Horse.

The reasons are basic. The rippling muscles of the heavy horse bring an atavistic thrill to a civilization accustomed to unseen power controlled by a switch. To watch the sinews of a Shire or Clydesdale tauten in the traces is to realize the massive strength exerted by true horse-power.

And instead of those offensive petrol fumes there is the pungent aroma of horse manure. It is valuable stuff, as gardeners, especially mushroom and rose growers, know. The 'stable smell' is a unique and

*Whitbread's four-horse hitch of grey Shires on parade.*

nostalgic compound of horse manure, clover hay, harness oil and leather; its property is to induce conversation among all those under its influence, and much of the countryside's deepest lore has been spread in the stable of an evening.

The heavy horse stable has sounds all its own. The great hooves clomp-clomp on cobblestones brushed to breakfast-table cleanliness, horses blow into their mangers, sending up little plumes of chaff and rattling the block of salt lick which helps keep their coats bright. Sweet-smelling hay is pulled, rustling, from the rack, and the mangel wurzel fed in some stables rolls along the manger.

Competition to have the fittest pair of horses on the place often led to outbreaks of thieving. But I doubt if any gods of the stable would condemn it; the pilfering took the form of illicit visits to the farm granary, to gain extra oats with which to feed the farmer's own horses. It is yet another example of the care and devotion lavished on the great teams, and the love for them borne by the men who attended them.

Now those stable sounds, sights and smells that seemed to have vanished for ever are returning. Horses are being used on the land again. Their return is slow, but on small farms, on difficult land and where large teams

Left, above *Horses must be trained to go back as well as forwards!*

Right *As though drawn with a ruler, these ploughing match furrows are the culminating art of horsemanship. If a man can plough like this, he can do anything with a team, hence the continued interest in horse ploughing.*

Left *Charlie Pinney bindering with a pair of Ardennes. This squat but powerful breed has recently been introduced to Britain from the Continent.*

Potatoes on this Lincolnshire farm are led off by horse and cart when the land is too wet to carry a mechanical harvester. In some autumns the horses have been the sole means of saving thousands of pounds' worth of crop.

of horses can be yoked together, it is happening.

A man with a pair of horses can plough an acre a day. With a large tractor and multi-furrow plough he turns over six or ten times as much – the intensive work occurs in the factory, not on the land. Now six or eight horses are being yoked as one team, to plough with more than one furrow and with a seat for the driver.

An enterprising agricultural engineering venture based at the Cotswold Farm Park has brought out horse-drawn machinery in modern materials. Manure spreaders for two horses, fertilizer spinners, hay turners and cultivating implements are now available, resolving the chicken-and-egg situation under which farmers didn't use horses because all their implements were out-of-date, and no manufacturer dared make them because so few horses worked on the land.

There are now farm; where most of the power is horse-supplied, yet where at least as much money is earned from leasing teams to advertising agents. If a firm desires to launch a new product or open a new branch, how much more impressive to herald it from a brightly painted dray hauled by a pair of black Shires with eight shining white legs, or a team of bright chesnut Suffolks?

*Eddie Dore with a pair of Percherons and corn seed drill. Drilling straight and true ranks high in the horseman's art, as the seam rows show any deviation when the corn comes through.*

11

# The Breeds

### The Shire

Of the four main British breeds, there are more Shires than any other – now between five and ten thousand horses with classes for them at 200 shows. So wherever you go in England and Wales, Shires will be within easy range. In Scotland and Northern Ireland, Clydesdales prevail.

A Shire stallion may stand eighteen hands high at the shoulder, and as a hand is four inches, that is more than the average man's height. A horse of nineteen hands – and there are a few – requires a medium-sized man to stretch up his arm to the point on the shoulder at which all horses are measured.

The height of a horse can quickly be assessed: first, measure from the ground to various points on your face. The height of your chin, nose, eyebrows, or forehead top can be ascertained against a door at home and measured; and then when a Shire is met in brewer's dray or on showground, its height may be gauged by standing alongside it and holding up a hand level with the wither. It is a professional's trick that most can learn, but ask the groom's permission first; a side-stepping Shire is awfully heavy!

The colours acknowledged by the Shire Horse Society are black, brown, bay and grey. Piebald or chestnut are no longer accredited Shire colours, to the regret of some for whom variety is the spice of life. In the early days, both colours existed.

In the 1970s, black became the most fashionable colour. At the Shire Horse Society's spring show at Peterborough, horse after horse could be seen of solid black, apart from a white blaze down the face and two, three and often four white legs.

This combination of contrasting colours is undoubtedly attractive. Also, black is black, and therefore easily matched. Bay and brown appear in various shades, so it is less easy to assemble matched teams. However, today there has been a swing back to brown and bay, the latter being a shade of brown with black mane and tail. A brown horse has mane and tail that matches its body colour, but the body colour should be deep and solid, not roan or splatched with white.

Grey is a historic Shire colour. It remains popular, though has lost some ground since the 1940s. Grey too can be of various shades; iron grey, steel grey and dapple grey are all found. Greys tend to go whiter with age, and a light-coloured horse is difficult to keep clean, so modern labour-saving tendencies do not favour the colour. But it contrasts well with a green waggon, and a pair of well-matched grey Shires in a plough is among the finest sights on Earth.

One feature easily identifies Shires and Clydesdales. They have 'feather' or hair on the lower legs, while Suffolks and Percherons are 'clean legged'. Around the turn of the century the feather on a Shire became an

*Hay turning is a job well suited to horse power, as shown by this active Shire.*

13

The busy collecting ring scene shown over the head of this Shire stallion is replicated a hundred times during the summer.

obsession for breeders, and was quite impractical on clay soils as the legs became impossible to keep clean. One result of labour-saving ideas is the breeding of finer, more silky hair, though this is roundly condemned by the old-school Shire enthusiast.

In popular legend the Shire is descended from the great horse of war as used by medieval knights. Suits of armour indicate that the war horses would be classed as strong cobs today, and did not attain the massive size usual among Shires doing the heaviest work in the late nineteenth century. Teams in the Liverpool docks then had enormous bone and strength.

As a farm and town horse, the Shire was being systematically bred even before the formation of its breed society in 1878, and the compilation of its first stud book.

We owe much to those early scribes who delved deep into the breeding of their favourite animals, as far as the memory of man allowed. For instance, the grey Champion 373 was foaled in 1802, bred by J. Jackson, Wilmslow, Cheshire, and sold to John Dray at Mobberley, Knutsford, Cheshire. His sire was the brown Ploughboy 1719 – numerical order did not follow age in those first stud books – based at Bollin Hall, Cheshire, and foaled in 1785. *His* sire was the Wiltshire Brown Horse (Summerland's) and

*Clydesdales wearing Scottish peaked collars. The scene is the Scottish National Ploughing Match. The reins or strings that guide the team are looped safely from back band to collar.*

A splendid team of
Clydesdales at Levin,
New Zealand, owned
by Mr J. G. Cottle.
The arrangement of
swingletrees or
baulks behind the
horses enables their
power to be hitched to
a central point on the
disc harrows.

there end our efforts to part the mists of time.

Two centuries later the Shire is stepping out confidently to meet the needs of the eighties. Backed by an enterprising breed society, it has brought blood testing and other modern refinements into its breeding programmes. It is sought by hoteliers, contractors, engineers, professional people and many from other walks of life who demand a worthwhile hobby. Shire breeding gives that and more.

## The Clydesdale

In terms of numbers, the Clydesdale reached its peak, as did other heavy breeds, in the early 1920s. Clydesdale Stud books for 1919, 1920 and 1921 have a combined thickness of almost seven inches, and contain the registrations of 5000 mares and 700 stallions. There were of course thousands more unregistered Clydes.

Scotland's heavy horse had by then spread to most English-speaking countries, Australia being a Clydesdale stronghold.

When Scotsmen emigrated, they naturally took with them their most familiar form of power.

Today Clydesdale and Shire are not too easily distinguishable. In fact, a few years ago one had to be something of a horseman to tell the difference, but the two breeds are once more setting their own standards.

Lively action has always been a sought-after Clydesdale characteristic. Its hind-leg action is such as to remind the onlooker of a Scotsman wearing his kilt with a bit of a swagger!

Colours of the breed are black, brown, bay, grey or roan. There are few grey Clydesdales, and more roans than breeders really like to see, for the 'hard' colours of bay and brown are preferred. White legs and a white blaze or face are Clydesdale characteristics, and the feather should be fine and silky. Northern horsemen set great store by this fineness of feather.

There are some most attractive blue roans, and also blacks with white socks, but the bright bay is probably the most sought after.

The basis of the modern Clydesdale was a sound native horse, active yet short in the leg. On these, Black Flanders and English Shire stallions were used, and there is a disputed legend that in the late seventeenth century the Duke of Hamilton introduced six black Flemish stallions onto his estates.

Around 1715 or 1720, John Paterson of Lochlyoch brought in a black Flemish stallion from England, and set up a Clydesdale stud. A hundred years later, we have the written records of the First and Retrospective Volume of the Stud Book which, though published in 1878, lists horses bred as far back as could be ascertained. Lofty 453, a light brown, was foaled in around 1825, and his bright bay sire, Old Stitcher, around 1818.

The breed was really established from 1865 to 1925. By the end of this period, the

Clydesdale was a different animal from the heavier-legged, heavier-feathered Shire with whom it had common ancestry.

A series of outstanding sires helped build the Clyde. The first of the period was Darnley, foaled in 1872, and described by leading breeder William Dunlop as having 'the most beautiful, well-placed and well set-on neck and head that I have ever seen in a draught horse. His produce [offspring] had plenty of bone and hair, a big, deep, wide carcass on short legs, and with big quarters.'

Prince of Wales was another to set his seal on Clydesdale breed type. Baron's Pride, Hiawatha, Sir Everard, Top Gallant and Bonnie Buchlyvie were names bandied about the Scottish countryside in late Victorian and Edwardian times. All had their advocates, but no horse of any breed was so prolific a stallion as Dunure Footprint.

Born in 1908, Dunure Footprint won every

*Compare this heavy-legged Clydesdale with the modern types. Prince of Wales and Darnley (foaled 1872) both played a great part in stabilizing the Clydesdale breed, and implanting upon it the freedom and action for which it became world famous.*

*Percherons are found
in different shades of
grey, with the
occasional white
animal, and also black.
A white foot or white
star or blaze on the
face is permitted.*

possible trophy. In the 1917 Stud Book, 146 foals by him are registered. Taking into account deaths, non-registrations and mares that were not fruitful, the claim that he covered over 300 mares a season is valid. And his service fee was £120, almost twice a man's wage for a year. At the season's height he served a mare every two hours, day and night, and two cows were kept solely to provide him with milk.

Clydesdales continued to provide farm and town power throughout the twenties and thirties – then came the war and mechanization.

An outbreak of the dreaded grass sickness in northern Scotland speeded the demise of the Clydesdale as a main power source. Its numbers became very small, and diminished still further through exports. Now it is booming again, with a re-invigorated breed society, and a nucleus of very keen breeders throughout Scotland, northern England and Northern Ireland.

## The Percheron

Black or grey, and very occasionally white, the Percheron does not share the long history of the other heavy breeds in Britain. Yet its story is interesting enough. It was developed in an area south-east of Paris known as Le Perche, and included in its numbers both strong carriage horses and heavyweights.

With its clean limbs almost free from feather, it is easy to picture the Percheron as a coach horse. It found favour overseas, particularly in North America, before becoming well known in Britain, where it arrived in a roundabout way.

During World War I, the horse-minded British Tommies were supplied with trans-Atlantic teams, the North American continent being raked for suitable animals. These included a fair sprinkling of Percherons, whose adaptability and temperament so impressed the soldiers that they determined to try them at home in more peaceful times.

So the breed was introduced to Britain and a stud book established. The British Percheron Horse Society has its headquarters and lively annual show at Cambridge. It is a friendly club, and Percheron prices are not so high as those of more fashionable breeds, so it is ideal for new starters.

Arab influence generations ago has left its mark on the Percheron's refined head and action. It is claimed to be the town horse par excellence, for its hard blue hooves have been bred to withstand the wear and tear of the French pavés, and now the tarmac of English cities as it delivers loads of beer.

Though the body is active, the placid temperament has been retained by judicious

*Percheron mare and foal. All foals are born black, even though their adult colour may be grey. The eventual colour is best judged at the extremities, especially around the nose.*

selection and handling. It is not uncommon for a Percheron stallion to be driven in a team of mixed sexes, and no breed needs less introduction to the hazards, noise and smell of city traffic.

Another advantage is that fresh blood may be introduced from across the Channel. British breeders go over to France, drink the wine and return with a consignment of Percherons to open up new strains. The imports stand out, as they usually carry more flesh than is customary among British-bred stock. They are being incorporated to advantage into the British studs.

The breed found favour overseas due to its clean legs, for the weeds of the prairies contained burrs which were a great nuisance to hairy-legged Shires. There are still over 1500 pedigree stallions, mares and fillies in Canada, where geldings are not registered. The Percheron gelding did well in hot climates due to its heat-resisting grey colour.

Height standards are not less than 16.3 hands for stallions and 16.1 hands for mares. The present demand is for tall, showy animals to take the judge's eye rather than the lower-slung horse whose point of draught is more suited to field work.

The Percheron Saltmarsh Silver Crest figures in the *Guinness Book of Records* as the heaviest horse in Britain at almost 25 cwt (2800 lb). His grandson Pinchbeck Union Crest stood 18 hands 2½ inches high at ten years old, yet was as nimble as a cat. Of such is Percheron history made.

### The Suffolk

No breed of heavy horse has advanced as much as the Suffolk in recent years. Classes filled with level, well-bred and well-fed animals have been the rule recently, whereas ten years ago it was difficult to reach double figures. Nor is there any suggestion of outside blood in this breed, for it is Britain's only chesnut breed (so spelt by Suffolk people) and the tightly-knit circle of East Anglian breeders saw to the maintenance of purity. One progenitor of the modern Suffolk, Crisp's Horse, was advertised at stud as 'a five year old, to get good stock for coach or road, a fine bright chesnut, full 15½ hands, noted for getting remarkably fine colts'.

That was in 1773, when the state of the roads demanded weight. In its earlier days the breed's foot conformation left something to be desired, but breeders, realising this, instituted foot classes judged by competent farriers. The result was a selection of stallions with sound feet, and greater care of foot health, and today the Suffolk can claim feet as sound as any breed.

Although regarded as an agricultural horse, the East Anglian breed is now used for city pageants of all kinds. It is a mighty puller, and the low point of draught gives the Suffolk an advantage over taller horses in the pulling competitions. At Soham Show, 1977, a Suffolk gelding harnessed to a sledge pulled 1 ton 2½ cwt from a dead pull, breaking all British records for this event.

The Suffolk has been fortunate in its Society officers. The author of the first stud book, the redoubtable Herman Biddell, not only compiled an invaluable and unbelievably detailed breed history, but bred Suffolks as well, and set the style for long-serving officers. Mr Wilfred Woods, who died in 1979, had served in the Woodbridge office for 60 years!

Its clean legs and chesnut colour make the Suffolk an admirable horse from which to breed heavyweight hunters. Both the Thoroughbred/Suffolk cross and the three-

Right *The hitch-cart, a seat on wheels that may be attached to a variety of implements. It is really safer if it runs behind. These Percherons are pulling a heavy Cambridge roller.*

*The method of plaiting the mane of this magnificent Suffolk stallion is clearly seen. All the hair is taken into the plait, whereas in Shires only part is used, and the rest combed down. The gold and scarlet ribbon enhances the appearance of the neck.*

quarter Thoroughbred/one-quarter Suffolk make first-class police horses or heavyweight hunters. There has always been a shortage of that class of animal, and the temptation to breed the lucrative first cross can result in a shortage of pure breeding stock.

Today there are 150 to 200 Suffolk horses in the USA. In 1955-6 three stallions and 47 mares were exported to Pakistan, to found a breeding programme for Mountain Artillery work, and a further 17 horses were taken in the two succeeding years.

# Horse Names

Those early heavy horse stud books reflect the history of the British Countryside. The first four volumes of Shire genealogy include 40 Ploughboys or Ploughmans! There are nine Admirals and no less than 80 Draymans, a name seldom heard today. No fewer than 16 pages with the prefix Honest are found, chiefly Honest Tom, with 22 Nelsons and, surprisingly, nine Napoleons. What's Wanted has endured until today, but only two are found in the first volume.

Black Beauty did not stray often into the range of Shire names, but Bonny and Blossom occur on page after page. Smiler was a favourite, and Lightsome. Gypsy and Flower were both well liked, as was Diamond, the name of a Shire mare that I drove when she was over 30.

Breeders went to town more with the stallion names. Farmer, Farmer's Friend and Farmer's Profit are all well liked, and there are even two Farmer's Supports, both from County Durham. England's Glory appears 56 times.

In our own day, Shire stallions include Nijinsky, Jubilee Monarch and Jubilee Prince, Telstar, Jet, Playboy and Goldfinger. But

*The Percheron stallion Willingham Andrew, in front of a packed grandstand. Breed headquarters are at Cambridge, where a special welcome is offered to newcomers to the heavy horse world.*

there are still the Squires, Grey Princes, Challengers and Gallant Lads. Among contemporary female Shires are Glamour Girl, Queen Elizabeth, Hat Trick and Modern Maid, with only a sprinkling of the old-time Duchesses, Diamonds, Bonnies and Beauties.

One breeder decided that it was time the name Courage was used in the Shire world. He bred a foal brown as Courage's Beer – and thought of the wonderful dressage horse Dutch Courage, and also of a Hackney stallion with few peers, Buckley Courage. So the colt was duly christened and soon had to live up to his name in fighting off a navel infection while still suckling. He did, and Ladbrook Courage went on to win the major foal show of 1980 at Stafford.

The Suffolk Stud Book brings in the tang of East Anglia with Rushmere and Marsh Boy. Cup-bearer is a traditional Suffolk name, and Sandy and Sunflower would hardly be used for Percherons.

*Geoffrey Morton's eight-horse team pulling gang rollers and harrows, and using a hitch-cart. More horses may be seen in the background on these East Riding acres.*

*Opposite A kindly pair of Suffolk heads. The start of the neck plaiting is clearly seen. Suffolks generally have excellent temperaments, and their colour is always one of seven shades of chesnut.*

General Gordon was a Suffolk stallion foaled in 1883, while Raglan, Lord Randolph, Lord of the Harem and Harvester are others found.

Modern Suffolks include Marshland Piper, Cherrytrees Lady Sheila and Rose Cottage Rosalind. Colony is another Suffolk prefix, from Hollesley Bay Colony, now part of HM Prison Service where the heavy horses play a positive part in helping wayward youngsters find a role in life.

*Before one can work a horse, it must be caught. These Shires near Scarborough, Yorkshire, are more amenable than some, for a horse that cannot readily be caught is an abomination.*

In over 60 years of British history, the Percheron has stamped its own character on heavy horse nomenclature. Bred chiefly in East Anglia, it has acquired regional prefixes – Fen, Pinchbeck, Three Holes and Willingham.

Pinchbeck Union Crest was one of the most famous breed stallions, with Hales Andromeda a well-known mare. From time to time French names appear, as evidence of recent imports: Etoile, Hostesse, Lutige and Hunotte-de-Courtangis.

If the Percheron reflects Continental influence, and the Shire is part of Old England, there is no doubt about the origin of Clydesdale names. Bonnie Doon, Auchindarroch Bell, Garthy Chieftain and Duke of Perth are Scottish to the core, as are Rob Roy, Rovin' Charlie and Laird o' Logan.

Highland Chief and Highland Laddie are in the 1879 Retrospective Volume. By 1921, a year of peak registrations, three full columns of Maggies and two of Kates are found, while Lainshaw Pride, Knight of the Borders, Caledonia and Celtic Guard need little detective work to track down their country of origin.

Today Footprint crops up among Clydesdales, a reminder of that most famous sire Dunure Footprint, pre-eminent around the time of World War I.

*Two grey Percherons drilling corn.*

# Vehicles

A *cart* is basically a two-wheeled vehicle drawn by one horse. It may be tipped by removing a pin, and pushing the load upwards aided by the horse's backing movement. It has an end door, removed before tipping, side boards, front board and back board which add to capacity by raising the sides by about ten inches.

Other attachments include shelvings, a light though strong framework which adds to the cart's surface area for comparatively light substances such as hay, straw or sheaves of corn. In front of and behind the shelvings, racks are fitted to extend upwards and assist the loader in his task of making a safe and tidy load of hay or sheaves.

The traditional cart is iron-tyred, but most newer ones have pneumatic tyres. Shafts must be strong, and are fitted with metal eyes near the front of each to take trace chains. These are used only when an extra heavy load is being pulled uphill, the trace horse being tied behind for the rest of the journey. Its traces are kept apart by a *stretcher*, a length of wood which prevents the chains chafing the horse's flanks.

A *waggon* has four wheels. Its design varies according to its county of origin. Most waggons were built south of the Scottish Border, and distinctive styles include the Wolds waggon, with a pole rather than shafts. On the steep slopes of the Yorkshire Wolds a load of corn might tip over, and less damage to horses and vehicle occurred with a pole rather than the less flexible shafts.

On the flat lands, waggons were bigger and more capacious. The Suffolk waggon was some 12 feet long, four feet wide and two-and-a-half feet deep. The heavier type was used for taking sacks of corn to the mill or merchant, wheat being in 16 or even 18 stone sacks, so it was not difficult to amass a big load.

Such a waggon would be used when a married farmworker moved house. It was also the conveyance for the mortal remains of a farmer or farm worker, and many landowners have expressed a wish that their last ride be made on a farm waggon. For such occasions, brasses were cleaned, and either a favourite horse or a team of blacks harnessed. In more than one instance, all the farm horses in fields abutting the funeral march have lined the fences, intuitively realising that this was no ordinary load.

The Sussex type of waggon was almost 14 feet long, and narrower at the front to allow the wheels to lock round. It stood almost six feet high at the rear, and six inches less at the front. The Hampshire waggon was very similar.

A waggon loaded with sheaves of corn has often been likened to a sailing ship – 'those towering galleons of gold' as David B. Nixon termed them. None was more beautiful than the Oxfordshire or Woodstock type, with its curving rails rising over the rear wheels. The

*In the woods: Ann
Williams clearing
timber on her
Saddlescombe farm,
Kent. The stretcher
keeping apart the trace
horse's chains is clearly
shown. When fully
loaded, the driver
walks beside the shaft
horse's head, and
drives the trace horse
with long reins.*

A turn-out class at a country show. Wooden wheels and iron tyres (left) generally score over rubber tyres in the show ring.

Berkshire type was of this design, but smaller. Wiltshire and Gloucester waggons had very high but narrow rear wheels.

We are fortunate in seeing these waggons today, for such was the excellence of the craftsmanship and the seasoning of the timber that they have endured for a century and more. Other farm implements have rusted or become outmoded, which has put a brake on the horse's renaissance on the land.

Now some Polish machines have been imported, and a modern fertilizer-spreader with a glass-fibre spinner is proving useful. Manure-spreaders and hay-turners are also being developed for horses, and light, manoeuvrable carts and rulleys.

The terms *rulley* and *dray* are used loosely for four-wheeled vehicles. A rulley is generally flat, with no more than a low rim, and would be used for delivering coal and goods in sacks.

*Pulling match. The sledge is loaded with concrete blocks of known weight, and the horse to pull most over the 27 ½ feet distance is the winner. No whips are allowed. Here a Shire gives his all.*

A brewer's dray has a seat, giving the coachman a vantage point above his team.

Some of today's most biddable horses work in woods. Timber extraction is a job at which they excel, and foresters assert that a well-trained horse does far less damage to young trees than any mechanical contrivance. A single horse can haul quite sizeable trunks to the roadside. His constant journeyings forward and back result in a considerable harvest by nightfall.

A recent development is the use of horse-drawn vehicles for advertising. In the early 1900s, billboards and sign-writing were used on trade vehicles, but were rather lost in the throng. Today, a team of heavy horses in a city centre is a rarity, and everyone takes notice.

The grey Percherons stepping through crowded Sunderland streets not only deliver beer for Vaux Breweries, but make passers-by look up at the clip-clop of hooves, a welcome change in a mechanical world. Across the Pennines in Blackburn, Thwaites are equally well known for their teams of Shires, as are the Ram Brewery at Wandsworth, and Courage's Shires.

Others to help the heavy horse boom include Bass, Coalite and Ind Coope. State Express is but one firm to hire a team for shows and pageants, and the chesnut Suffolk contrasting with a green-and-gold waggon makes a particularly inspiring sight.

*More traditional use of the heavy in a Northamptonshire village. The horse learns where to stop, and walks forward of its own accord when spoken to by the driver. Horse power has much to recommend it for any retail round.*

*Opposite One of the fine old waggons saved from the breaker's. The hoop-raved style which sweeps over the rear wheel was extensive over the south Midlands and the south and west.*

*Single-horse turn-outs line up before the judges at Peterborough.*

In Glasgow, Buchanans use what is probably Britain's tallest horse, Chester, standing well over 19 hands high, to deliver Black & White Whisky. No prizes for guessing the horse's colours, but whether the heavies are black, brown, bay, grey or chesnut, the rippling muscles and ringing hooves remain a perennial attraction.

# Harness and Decoration

The colossal power of the heavy horse is of no use to man unless it is harnessed. The verb has been borrowed for steam, mechanical and even nuclear power, but basically horse harness is a means of both using and guiding the animal's strength.

The *collar* fits around the shoulders, and the horse thrusts into it. Despite all the modern synthetic materials available, none has yet been found to replace wheat straw for packing the collar. The straw absorbs the sweat and helps prevent sore shoulders. Fitting the collar is a skilled job; if too tight, the animal cannot breathe property, and if slack it will rub and injure the skin.

*Hames* of wood or metal fit round the collar, hooked at the bottom and strapped at the top. Each hame has a hame hook onto which trace chains are hung, thereby enabling forward power to be applied. The hames also have a ring on each side, through which the reins are threaded to prevent them trailing.

If a horse is pulling a shafted implement, such as a hayrake, or a cart, it needs a *saddle*. The chains from the hames will pull the implement forward, but the shafts must be supported. So a well padded saddle with a bridge to take the backchain is strapped on by means of the girth.

Each saddle is fitted with *breechings*. This is leather webbing passing round the haunches, and strapped to the back of the saddle. If the horse has to brake its load on a downhill slope, it leans back into its breechings, which are chained to the shafts. Similarly, if a stationary load must be reversed, this is achieved by the horse backing into its breechings. Implements such as ploughs and harrows that are worked purely through chains cannot be backed.

When driving in chains rather than shafts, a *back band* or strap of leather or webbing supports the chains on either side. The *trace chains* stretch from the hames to the *swingletrees* which are hitched directly or indirectly to the implement being pulled. There are many regional variations for these terms.

In pole harness, one horse stands on either side of a long pole, and the draught is via the traces. The pole has a cross-piece at the front to which leather straps are fitted. These slip through the bottom of the collar, thus supporting the pole. The vehicle or implement is steered via the pole, and it helps backing or braking.

Though the horse is now equipped to move the implement, the manoeuvre is useless unless the power is controlled. The bridle on the horse's head is fitted with a *bit* that passes through the mouth, with a ring at each end.

It is said that 'there is a key to every horse's mouth', but a well-schooled heavy should need little more than a simple, straight bit.

Most bridles for heavies are fitted with blinkers, blinders or, as the manufacturers termed them, winkers. These are solid flaps of

*Ploughing, with the dog following. Farm dogs had a much more companionable time in the horse days, when they could lie on their owner's coat on the headland under the hedge, and join him when they pleased.*

*Gavin Cole restoring a cart saddle near Brancepeth, Crook, Co. Durham. Much harness was thrown away in the 1950s, and though some is beyond recall, oil and careful work can perform wonders.*

leather which prevent the horse from seeing behind him. Their use is open to question, and the *open bridle* has none.

While at work the horse may retain its *halter*, the shank of which is tied to its own or its partner's collar. Where two or more horses are worked abreast, they are hitched to their neighbour by a *coupling band* from bit to bit.

The driver's *reins* (of leather) or *strings* (of rope) run from the bit ring through rings on collar or traces so as to give the most direct line. On no account are they tied to the implement, as the horses' mouths could be severely damaged in case of an accident.

*Every link in every chain must be bright and clean to stand a chance in the modern show scene.*

*Although most of the decorated harness is functional, such items as the breastplate, neck strap and rein hanger are mainly ornamental.*

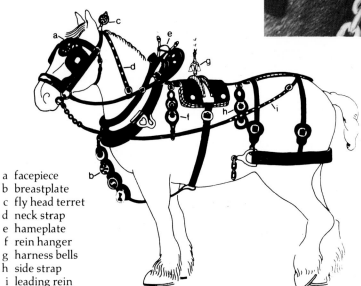

a facepiece
b breastplate
c fly head terret
d neck strap
e hameplate
f rein hanger
g harness bells
h side strap
i leading rein

## Harness Decorations

The non-brass decorations are of two main types, woollen and floral. They seem to have developed in Scotland from displays of ribbons and flowers used for high days and holidays before World War I. The decorations were first applied to mane and tail but then spread to the harness.

The next step was to add to the basic harness decoration by wire frames on the saddle and breeching. These frames are termed the bridge and the crown, and a certain degree of standardisation has occurred.

Classes now distinguish between floral and woollen types. Paper flowers were first used, and though fresh flowers have been fitted on occasion, their tendency to wilt and suffer from a summer shower has made the wearing of plastic flowers almost universal in this class.

Plastic flowers have no scent, however, and one very successful exhibitor told me that he always used fresh flowers of a particular scent when two ladies were judging!

In the woollen classes, coloured pom-poms and sprays are the main features. These are made on winter evenings, often by ploughmen and their families, rivalling as an art the intricately carved crooks of the hill shepherds.

## Plaiting

Plaiting of the mane and tail are other major skills. Styles vary with breeds. Only part of the hair of a Shire mane is incorporated in the plait, whereas with the Suffolk it is all taken in. Tail decorations also vary. Laws prohibiting docking of horses' tails have led to changes in the style.

The flags or standards surmounting the neck plait add to the horse's height, and a neck ribbon enhances the length of neck in a mare. A clever artist can make a rather flat-necked stallion appear proudly arched. By decking out the tail, it can seem to be better set than the reality. Ribbon and raffia are used partly because horse hair on its own is slippery, and does not remain in knots.

## Brasses

The best known horse decorations are of course brasses. The author Terry Keegan tells us that the practice of wearing horse brasses on farms began quietly enough, and

*Putting the finishing touches to a Clydesdale.
The bench is used to reach the higher
decorations. A tall heavy horse may be over
18 hands high, or six feet at the shoulder.*

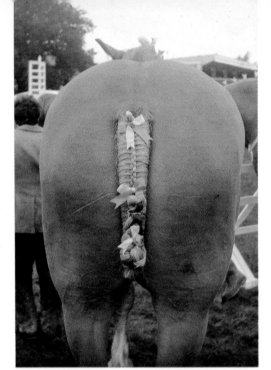

*The braiding of a Suffolk tail. Each breed has its own style of dressing, and the Suffolk's tail hair is left long, and then plaited with bows as shown.*

only reached its peak in the 50 years from 1870 to 1920. There is no evidence to suggest that, in the nineteenth and twentieth centuries at any rate, brasses were fitted to ward off evil spirits. They were chosen for their prettiness or ease of cleaning.

Heavy horse harness has any amount of room on which to hang brasses. The first to appear was the face piece, hung by a special strap from the brow-band. Easily removed, it was generally kept for special occasions.

A whole series of brasses could be accommodated on the breastplate, a strap joining girth and collar. Studded straps showed hearts, ovals, crescents, diamonds and several other patterns. A North American speciality is the crossed face strap, fitting from brow-band to nose-band, and studded.

Horse brass collecting is a hobby in its own right. It has its own society, a number of public houses display admirable collections

*Horse brasses were sold in vast numbers in late Victorian times. The patterns shown here are fairly typical, for horses and wild animals were commonly featured, as well as geometric patterns.*

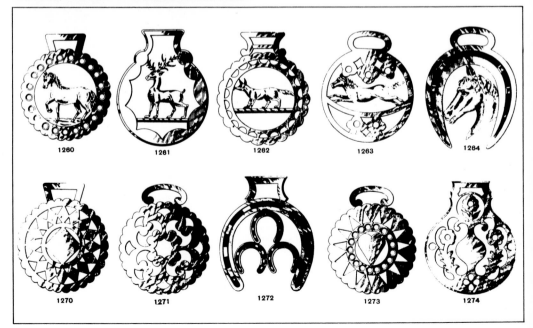

and some very high prices are realised for the rarer old sorts. Further details are given at the end of the book.

It is difficult even for the expert to date horse brasses. Brasses of modern origin may be skilfully doctored so as to appear old and partly worn. Design, colour, file marks, the amount of wear and patina are all taken into account, but something is learnt from each, and the collector's hobby can become a fascinating one.

For the enthusiast who does not wish to spend vast sums building up a collection, there is much to be said for collecting modern brasses. There is then no pretence. Over 30 new brasses were struck to mark the Silver Jubilee of Queen Elizabeth II.

Another possibility is to collect other metal horse decorations. Heavy horses are decked out with bells, brass-cased hames, fly head terrets, and a whole range of buckles.

Even the knobs surmounting the hames

*No foot, no horse. The skilled farrier sees to it that every horse walks as well as possible. This popular demonstration is at the Doncaster Pageant of the Horse.*

*A pair of Percherons ploughing at a working demonstration.*

are in various patterns. Some beautiful modern bells are made, and the throng round a supplier's stall at a heavy horse show proves the general interest.

For those who love the heavy horse, but lack the time or space to keep one, a hobby such as brass or harness decoration collecting has much to commend it. It brings one into the heavy horse world, while a tasteful collection can appreciate in value and cost little in storage. For, as Mr Jorrocks said: 'Confound all presents wot eats!'

# The Heavy Horse Abroad

The two-horse team was the most common power unit in Britain for most cultivating operations – ploughing, dragging, harrowing, drilling, rolling. Both size of field and the large number of skilled men available discouraged bigger teams, while in the inter-War depression, farmers had no money to spend on new machinery to displace a trusted worker on 32s a week.

In the New Countries things were very different. Fields were often vast, skilled horsemen very much at a premium, while large numbers of horses could be kept cheaply.

Nor was there such a conservative attitude to work. A seat was normal when driving the big teams of Canada, USA, Australia and New Zealand. In Britain those stalwart foremen of the old school regarded such a fitting as 'encouraging idleness', and I have even been told to add sand bags to a roller needing extra weight and to walk, rather than fit a seat and give myself a ride over the half-brick clods!

The use of multiple hitches became almost an exact science in the USA and the former Dominions. Literal horse power was closely studied at the farm colleges. The placing of the six-, eight-, twelve-horse or even larger team was worked out mathematically. Elimination of side draft and such matters as freedom for work were studied closely.

The best farmers in the big-team sections of the American West used enough horses on each implement to allow them to cover 20 miles' productive work per ten-hour day. They ploughed a furrow when going out to work and another on the way home.

Occasionally teams walked at two-and-a-quarter miles an hour. Where implements such as harrows could not be fitted with a seat, they were provided with a hitch-cart or bogey. This was a light two-, three- or four-wheeled framework with seat attached, nothing more. Or the teamster might drive while riding a steady cob.

The horses were not all schooled and broken in, in the British sense. Canadian horsemen have told me that a horse was considered broken when it had worn a collar five or six times. Such niceties as learning to have their feet picked up were unheard of, and if a horse needed attention, it was probably hobbled and cast by ropes.

Horses are herd animals, and this factor is more responsible for the success of the big team than any other. The animals like being together, so they pack in behind the leaders and walk away with the rest. Sometimes they run away. Life with a big team is certainly never dull, but it is not five times more difficult to drive ten than to drive a pair.

The seat helps. The need to keep half one's mind on keeping one's feet while stumbling among the clods is removed. The reins go to the bits of outside lead horses, and not directly to others.

This is why top-class lead horses are so invaluable. They set the pace for the whole team. They stop it when in trouble, often through voice commands alone. The rest of the team is worked through a system of 'tying in and bucking back'.

Each tie has a snap fastener, for much time would be wasted by even the smartest tying of knots. One end is snapped into the halter ring of the horse in the rear; the other is snapped to the inside trace of the horse ahead. A horse thus 'tied in' must follow the leader.

Portable mangers and water troughs are used to avoid unyoking every individual animal at bait time. With the aid of such labour-saving devices, an eight-horse team can harrow 70 or 80 acres of corn a day.

Above *Another method of hitching the big team. Mr G. R. D. Barwell driving Mr R. L. Barwell's team in South Canterbury, New Zealand, in the mid-1970s. The hitch here is different from that shown on page 24 as the horses are yoked in two lines of four. More freedom of movement is afforded by such a method.*

Opposite *A pair of Belgians hauling a plough with seat attached. Belgians, usually of sorrel or chestnut colour, are very popular in North America. The harness decorations differ from the British type.*

*Horse gear working an elevator. Such shafting was employed to drive a variety of milling, mixing and other stationary equipment.*

One great advantage of a heavy horse team is its reserve of strength. A team of 18 can develop 180 horsepower for short periods when required. Then, when the going is easy, it can restore its energy for another hard pull. The mechanical term 'horsepower' is one of the most misleading ever conceived.

In Australia after World War I, tractors and fuel became cheap. There was no sale for horses, so they were simply turned loose by the dozen. Then came the slump, corn prices fell, and even cheap fuel was an expense the farm couldn't stand. The loose horses were caught and put back to work, for they consumed only stuff grown on the farm; there was no money to pay out. Who can say that a similar situation will not arise in the eighties?

*A Percheron team leaning into their collars in British Columbia. Leigh Cross of Hornby Island is leading hay bales from his meadows. Traces are leather, against the more usual British chains.*

47

# Art and Tradition

Throughout the great period of British sporting art in the late eighteenth and nineteenth centuries, the heavy horse received less then its due. Landowners and leading stockbreeders commissioned paintings of their playthings – hunters, hounds and dogs – and of prize-winning cattle and sheep likely to advertise their herds and flocks. The farm horse was so much part of everyday life that it was less frequently painted.

Examples may still be found, however, by diligent searching among the racehorses and hunters. Fores's *Series of the Mothers* depicts both a grey cart mare and a brown foal, and a beautiful dark bay draught mare and foal. Dated the mid-1850s, the prints are 'From the Original Picture by Mr J. F. Herring, Senr, in the possession of the Publishers'. The former depicts a stable scene, and the latter a pastoral with gate and stile. One may learn a great deal about the stamp of horse bred at the time, for these leading animal painters· both understood their subjects and had an eye for detail.

The more readily available smaller prints have regrettably been taken from books. One such is the Old Cart horse and the Improved Black Cart horse, published in 1804 by Richard Phillips, St Paul's Church Yard. The improved version has four white socks, but one can never be sure if this is a figment of the imagination of some later colourist.

One artist who made heavy horses his lifelong work was Luard (1872-1944). After studying art at the Slade, he did not find his perfect models until visiting Paris in 1904. He was entranced by the Percherons working in the streets and on the quays of the Seine.

The muscular make-up of the great animals fascinated him. Sometimes he sketched them as they worked, and sometimes he took home an image in his remarkable photographic mind of their movement and balance, as they shifted huge loads of stone or sand.

Luard's careful attention to the lines of power and motion is unquestionable. He conveyed the feelings of beauty, power, movement and even the willingness of the horses. He was one of the few painters who understood clearly the delicate mechanics of great power.

In the twentieth century, Lucy Kemp-Welch hung many lovely studies of working horses. A grey and black Shire in the autumn gold of a forest is a typical masterpiece. The way the hame rein hangs on the drooping resting neck, the number of links in the trace chain and the set of the blinkers are details sought by the heavy horse connoisseur.

They are all too often absent among modern artists, though the Misses D. M. and E. M. Alderson, of Darlington, and Geraldine Freeman, of Framlingham, Suffolk are notable exceptions. They know their horses because they have worked with them.

*Opposite A Kent waggon pulled by a decorated Shire.*

49

## Traditions

Secret societies of horsemen existed, especially in northern Scotland. Initiation came to a youngster in a barn in the middle of the night. He had to bring with him a loaf, a bottle of whisky and a candle; he was blindfolded, and led to an 'altar', often an inverted bushel measure pressed on a sack of corn.

Usually four horsemen were present, and various questions were asked of the novice, to which he had to give the correct answers. He then took the Horseman's Oath, part of which reads:

*Lovely detail by J. F. Herring Jnr. showing a Victorian farmyard. Harness details, as was usual with the horsemen/painters of the period, are authentic, and the going must have been heavy in view of the number of trace horses needed.*

Furthermore I vow and swear that I will never give it nor see it given to a tradesman of any kind except a blacksmith or veterinary surgeon or a horse-soldier. Furthermore I will never give it nor see it given to a farmer or a farmer's son unless he be working his own or his father's horses. Furthermore I will never give it nor see it given to my wife nor daughter nor yet to the very dearest ever lay by my side…
Furthermore I will never refuse to attend a meeting if warned within three days except in a case of riding fire or going for the doctor, and if I fail to keep these promises may my flesh be torn to pieces with a wild horse and my heart cut through with a horseman's knife and my bones buried on the sands of the seashore where the tide ebbs and flows every

Opposite *Ploughing in dry conditions.*

*At the Beamish Museum, Stanley, Co. Durham, sculptor Terry Coult works on a full size model of the Clydesdale stallion Silver Cup. The horse had more effect on local types than any other, for a fairly low-slung horse was favoured for the heavy work of this coal mining area. Silver Cup's height was estimated at 17.1 hands by taking angles against a groom's known height. Foaled in 1899.*

twentyfour hours so that there may be no remembrance of me amongst Lawful brethren so help me God to keep these promises. *Amen.*

After taking the Oath, the novice got a shake of the Devil's hand, a stick covered in hairy skin or a calf's foot. He was then given the Horseman's Word, of which one version was 'Both in one'.

It is easy to look lightly on these matters in

our computerized age. To the ill-educated, poverty-stricken youngster among much older men, at dead of night and dim lighting, the ceremony was often frightening and left a lasting mark, as indeed was intended.

Those who transgressed could have a fearful time. Powdered glass under their horses' collars ensured that the teams would not pull. Concoctions of aniseed were used to entice horses in what appeared a magical way. And much of the secret society lore remains secret, so fearful have the recipients remained over their fate if they divulged the information.

*A bay Clydesdale with white legs sets off the full brilliance of this Royal Highland Show scene.*

# The Future

Will the heavy horse return to the land in anything like its former numbers? World history gives us few grounds for thinking that this will be so, as man's sources of power tend to be replaced by something quite different. Wind or water power became outmoded, and if they are used in future the methods will be quite different from the old windmills and water wheels.

Modern farm machinery is so sophisticated that it is difficult indeed to visualize a complete return to animal power. Yet there are clear signs that for certain operations and particular soil types and conditions, the horse is returning.

It has the overwhelming advantage of breeding its own replacements. Leave two tractors in the same shed all winter, and in spring the result is depreciation of hefty capital investment. A mare taken to the

*The coachman of a pair of dapple-grey Shires acknowledging the crowd's applause at Peterborough.*

Clydesdales in the collecting ring. Fine, silky feather over the lower leg is a present-day feature. Though this scene is Ingliston, Edinburgh, the breed is also popular in Northern Ireland.

stallion in May has the chance of breeding a foal the following March that will be worth money in October, more still as a yearling, and a considerable amount if well looked after and broken to work from one to two years later.

The horse consumes farm produce. Its hay and oats are home-grown, and may provide a valuable break crop in an intensive arable rotation. Its vehicles are long-lasting and do not become outmoded. It provides manure for the land. Although it may cost several hundred pounds, the rate of increase is much less than with motor vehicles, whose increase in cost is five per cent every ninety days. Nor does the horse go slow, go on strike or refuse to work at weekends! Its working life may well be 12 or 15 years, twice that of a motor vehicle, at the end of which its hide, bones and flesh are still of value to mankind.

The horse has brains, which may be developed. It can learn to do jobs and to turn into the correct row of its own accord. I drove an aged Shire mare, Blossom, who did not know what it was to make a mistake. Yet her daughter Bonnie was a stupid tearaway. Breeding for brains and adaptability is an aspect sadly neglected by heavy horse people.

A one- or two-horse team is adequate for a great many farm jobs now done by a 65hp or even a 100hp tractor. The horse is safer on steep slopes, and though accidents in the horse days were not well tabulated, my impression is that there were fewer fatalities among horsemen than among tractor

*Spring is not spring without a foal in the paddock. Each of these Suffolk foals has been subject to plenty of care and attention, and showing at an early age is of lasting benefit. The youngster accepts crowds, noise, haltering and transport as normal.*

Opposite *Frieze of plough teams. The September scene is at Chertsey. The housens above the collars – a southern style of decoration – are seen on the far pairs. Their practical function is to prevent rain soaking down under the collar.*

*At the end of the day. Percherons at Vaux Brewery stable, Sunderland, receive their final grooming. A heavy horse stable has an atmosphere all its own.*

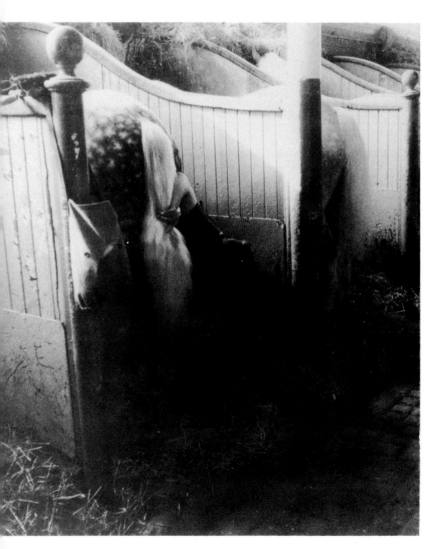

drivers, although a number of farm men limped through a kick from a horse.

Soil compaction is minimized when using a horse team. For short hauls – up to two or three miles – the horse has been proved more economical, which brings up the question of speed. One of the tractor's great assets, which applies to dales as well as lowland farms, is its ability to nip home quickly if plans change or something is forgotten. Nor does it take as much maintenance time as a horse team.

In addition, at the end of a hard winter, the tractor may be switched on and be ready for full work immediately. If horses have not been out regularly, they have to be 'fitted' or toned up like an athlete preparing for a race, and this takes time. When not at work, they still need feed and daily attention. If an engine part goes wrong, a spare can be obtained somehow. If a horse is sick or lame, rest may be part of the cure, and meanwhile the season is being lost. Epidemics can be very serious indeed.

Yet despite these drawbacks, the need for horses continues to grow, and sometimes in surprising ways. It was said that today's workers would not be prepared to put up with the tie of stable routine, but neither in town nor country has this proved to be the case. More and more youngsters are coming forward to work with horses, and the means of providing them with tuition and opportunities is a challenge of the twentieth century's last decades.

*No lack of activity in this ploughing scene. The bright red ear muffs are southern decorations.*

# Stallion Hiring Societies

Mobberley & District Shire Horse Society
(Secretary: F. R. Marshall)
36 Hawthorn Avenue, Wilmslow, Cheshire

Yorkshire Shire Horse Society
(Secretary: W. H. Chambers)
Trinity House Farm, Swanland Dale,
North Ferriby, East Yorkshire

Lichfield Shire Horse Society
(Secretary: R. F. Scoffham)
St Mary's Chambers, Lichfield, Staffordshire

Derbyshire Agricultural & Horticultural Society
(Secretary: B. G. Daykin)
17 Chestnut Avenue, Mickleover, Derbyshire

Great Eccleston Shire Horse Society
(Secretary: T. Kay)
c/o R. Mortimer, Fisher Farm, Longmeanygate,
Leyland, Preston, Lancashire

Montgomeryshire Entire Horse Society
(Secretaries: Morris, Marshall & Poole)
Coach Chambers, Welshpool, Powys

Wisbech Shire Horse Society
(Secretary: R. K. Reeve)
Agriculture House, Somers Road, Wisbech,
Cambridgeshire

Abergele & District Shire Horse Society
(Secretary: H. Thomas)
Garnedd, Llanfairfechan, Gwynedd

Hainton Horse Society
(Secretary: E. Cosgrave)
Northwalk Farm, Hainton, Lincolnshire

Lincolnshire Shire Horse Association
(Secretary: B. N. Neave)
School Lane, Grayingham, Gainsborough,
Lincolnshire

South/West Yorkshire Shire Horse Hiring Society
(Secretary: H. Lewis)
Goodyfield Farm, Tofts Lane, Rivelin, Sheffield,
S6 5SL

# Further Reading

Arnold, James, *All Drawn by Horses,*
    David & Charles, 1979
Chivers, Keith, *The Shire Horse,* J. A. Allen 1977,
    and Futura (abridged) 1978
CoSira., *The Blacksmith's Craft*

Ewart Evans, G., *Horse Power and Magic. The Pattern
    under the Plough. The Horse in the Furrow. The Farm
    and the Village. Where Beards Wag All. Ask the
    Fellows who Cut the Hay.* Faber 1970s
Hart, Edward, *Golden Guinea Book of Heavy Horses*

*Past and Present*, David & Charles 1976
Hart, Edward, *Showing Livestock*, David & Charles 1979
Hart, Edward, *The Heavy Horse*, Shire Publications 1979
Henschel, Georgie, *Horses and Ponies*, Kingfisher 1979
Lessiter, Frank *Horse Power*, Reiman Publications, Milwaukee, Wisconsin
Llewellyn Jones, John, *Schoolin's Log*, Michael Joseph 1980
Keegan, Terry, *The Heavy Horse: Its Harness and Harness Decoration*, Pelham Books, 1973
National Federation of Young Farmers Clubs, *Farm Horses*, 1940. Reprint Edward Hart Publications, The Yethouse, Newcastleton, Roxburghshire TD9 0TD, 1980
Oaksey, John, and Lord Snowdon, *Pride of the Shires*, Hutchinson 1979

Suffolk Horse Society, *The Suffolk Horse*, Church Street, Woodbridge, Suffolk, 1979
Telleen, Maurice, *Draft Horse Primer*, Rodale Press 1977
Thompson, John, A selection of facsimiles of carts, waggons and old farm implements. 1 Fieldway, Fleet, Hampshire
Weatherley, Lee, *Great Horses of Britain*, Saiga 1978
Weber Jepsen, *Heroes in Harness*, A. S. Barnes
Whitlock, Ralph, *Gentle Giants*, Lutterworth 1976

**Magazines**
*The Heavy Horse Magazine*
*Horse & Driving*, Watmoughs, Idle, Bradford
*Draft Horse Journal*, Waverly, Iowa 50677, USA
*The Evener*

# Breed Societies

British Percheron Horse Society
(Secretary: D. G. Maskell)
Owen Webb House, Gresham Road, Cambridge

Clydesdale Horse Society of Great Britain and Ireland
(Secretary: John Fraser),
c/o *Scottish Farmer*, 39 York Street, Glasgow C2 8JL

Shire Horse Society
(Secretary: Roy W. Bird, MBE)
East of England Showground, Peterborough

Suffolk Horse Society
(Secretary: P. Ryder-Davies)
Church Street, Woodbridge, Suffolk

**Horse Brasses**
National Horse Brass Society
(Secretary: J. R. Needham)
3 Holmwood Close, North Harrow, Middlesex AA2 6JX

**Supplies of Heavy Horse Brasses and Decorations:**
Terry Keegan, Country Centre, Clows Top, Kidderminster, Worcestershire

# Glossary

**Apron** Worn by all drivers of turnouts.

**Bay** Brown colour with black points (mane, tail and lower legs).

**Beam** Plough framework, to which the stilts or handles are attached.

**Bevelled Shoe** Slopes outwards from the hoof, to make the foot appear bigger.

**Blaze** White marking down front of face. A horse with a lot of white may be known as 'bald-headed'.

**Blinders, Blinkers** Leather eye shields on the bridle, preventing the horse from seeing behind.

**Breast** Curved part of the plough that turns the furrow. Also known as mouldboard.

**Breaking** Training to work with different types of equipment. A horse is 'broken to chains', i.e. harrowing or ploughing, before it is 'broken to shafts' or carting.

**Breeching, Britching** Heavy leather band with supporting straps, that fits round the horse's haunches and enables it to halt or back the vehicle.

**Bridle** Harness for the horse's head, including headstall and bit, and usually with a hame rein or short rein attached.

**Brood Mare** Used for breeding.

**By** Designates sire.

**Castrate** Make incapable of breeding; a castrated male usually has a quieter temperament.

**Chestnut** Small natural horny growth on inside of legs.

**Chestnut or Chesnut** Golden to deep red-brown colour, with tail and mane similar.

**Clean-Legged** Free of long hair or feather on lower legs. Percherons and Suffolks are clean-legged breeds.

**Collecting Ring** Adjacent to the showing ring, where exhibits meet just before entry.

**Colt** Young male horse, uncastrated.

**Coulter** Set in front of the mouldboard to make the plough's vertical cut.

**Draft, Draught** The former is the American version, but both mean the action of drawing or pulling.

**Dray** Four-wheeled vehicle, with seat. Brewers' vehicles are usually termed drays.

**Entire** Stallion.

**Felloes, Fellies** Sections of the circumference of the iron-tyred wooden wheel.

**Filly** Young female horse, word usually used in conjunction with age definition, e.g. filly foal.

**Furrow Horse** Offside horse; the right-hand one seen from the plough stilts. Some furrow horses are trained to walk just clear of the furrow, but retain their name.

**Gelding** Castrated male.

**Headland** End of the furrows, where the teams turn.

**High-cut** Unbroken furrow set on edge.

**In-hand** Synonymous with 'breed class'. Single animals shown, usually under breed society standards.

**Land Horse** Nearside horse; the left-hand one seen from the plough stilts.

**Mare** Female from three years onwards.

**Mouldboard** That part of the plough that turns the furrow over.

**Obstacle Test** Race against time by turnouts through a series of markers.

**Out of** Designates dam.

**Plough Body** *See* Breast.

**Point, Sock, Share** Detachable metal point that leads the plough body into the ground. It makes the horizontal cut. Plough points became rather a fetish among ploughmen, and before 1939 an incredible range was manufactured. These were standardized to three during World War II, to little detriment.

**Ridge, Rig** Start of a bout of ploughing, with two furrows set against one another.

**Seedbed** Fine, worked-down soil into which seed is drilled.

**Shank** Rope attached to a halter.

**Stallion** Male horse capable of breeding.

**Steward** Judge's assistant, there to carry out his wishes and facilitate his task.

**Swing** Ploughing without wheels.

**Swingletree** Piece of wood or metal with hooks, joining trace chains and implement, and holding the chains apart so that they do not chafe the horses' legs.

**Temperament** Natural disposition, e.g. fiery or placid.

**Trade Turn-Out** Normally applies to horses and vehicles used for deliveries or city work. Not farm vehicles.

**Turn-out** Vehicle plus horse in a show class. This is usually for single horse, pair, then three or four or more.

**Winkers** See Blinders

# Index

The numerals in **bold** type refer to the pages on which illustrations appear